The Ark
of
Lumijnfroost

The Ark

of

Lumijnfroost

A Menagerie of Verse

by Timothy Ray Phillips

Öpélaan Ïnktûr
Blacksburg, Virginia

ÖPÉLAÂN
Ï
ÏNKTÛR

Twaanévie Publishing House

ÖPÉLAAN

ÏNKTÜR

Twaanévie Publishing House
845 Deercroft Drive
Blacksburg, Virginia 24060
twaanevie_publishing@yahoo.com

Publisher's Cataloging-in-Publication Data
Phillips, Timothy Ray.
The ark of lumijnfroost: a menagerie of verse / Timothy Ray Phillips.
–1st ed.
p.   cm.
Poems.
Includes index.
ISBN 978-0-9660055-0-9
I.   Title
811'.54-dc23   2012912289

Printed in the United States of America

Also by Timothy Ray Phillips

Six Feet Under, Twelve Feet High
(How to Fight Post-Mortem Depression)

Between the Fog & the Freight Train

Timothy Ray Phillips

dedication

To Panadrew,
Home of the Lumijnfroost
and all Things good and natural

Thumpity-thump-thump.
The joy you never outgrow.
Little, grey Gumdrop.

The Ark of Lumijnfroost

Animaux de la plume

The Ark of Lumijnfroost

Mysteries lie
in the Irish forest,
the space between
my ancestral ears
when I hear
with a young heart
and watch the sparks
ignite like fireflies
after a summer wake

Timothy Ray Phillips
Between the Fog and the Freight Train

The Ark of Lumijnfroost

Timothy Ray Phillips

Enter the Ark...

The Ark of Lumijnfroost

ß01 Bones

These are the bones of a penman's heart—
creased lines laid bare of skin and nerve,
essence of the rib-caged soul preserved.
This is the ark where creatures impart
a glimpse of this human's condition.
Life prescribed in versed animation
where engaging eyes are words apart.

ß02 Penned Creatures

At the dark end

of the pen

come the liquid

curls and swirls,

elegant curves

over elephant trunks,

queues of regal souls.

Humps and double-humps,

the monkey-tailed y,

and crossback t.

The beady-eyed jay

that swoops down

and then carries away.

The b in the bonnet,

old u in the pasture,

the creatures of the open c;

they run and cover

the empty space.

Cheery o's that ease the flow
to the gee of the dogs,
and the eh
in the haw to the ox.
The determined dots
of the eye,
slanted to a wink—
Treasured jots,
the Inklings of wise
after-thought.
Peaks and valleys
that are the links
that move the mind
and stoke the heart.
Streaks and spots of ink
pressed in progressive lines.
Pre-destined patterns
finding shape
on paper blessed
with a watermark crest.

ß03 Sunrise

It is morning on Earth.
The giraffes are brushing
their necks toward
the blue african sky
as a cabbie waits anxiously
for his final fare to return.
A mama bear watches her cubs
roll head over heels down
a meadow still unknown.
In a Brooklyn brownstone

an elderly woman reads books

behind a door of many locks,

while seventeen crows alight

on a phone line near Hartford

that weighs heavy on a call

between a man and woman

Monkeys in a cage imagine

the rush and cries of jungle life

a toddler holds tight the spoon

of silver his mother gives him

as fires encroach the rain forest,

a little snow melts near Everest.

ß04 Rock of Ages

We once lay

unconscious

with blank minds

not yet made

to even

sleep.

Our bodies

lay like stones

in mason's

field—

> *head markers*
>
> *not yet raised*
>
> *or written*
>
> *on.*
>
> *Rock hard flesh*
>
> *without a*
>
> *name.*

From Heaven
He stepped down
at twilight
and breathed sharp
life into
us.
Our hearts jumped
and quivered;
the blood now
stirred.
We were at   *once*
     the quick
     among the
     dead
     with our eyes
     seeing the
     dark

          for the first
          time.

ß05 When Water Breaks

When water breaks
and the moon beams,
a new life begins.
A circle gathers
round the square bed
as the new mother
holds fast to the bond,
the tie that binds,
the mystic chord.
Unspoken word.
Quiet prayer
that this new life
would be greatly blessed
until its time to pass.

ß06 Uncut

At night,
when shades
are drawn,
I dance naked
in the park.
I am uncut,
wholly natural.
Ahead of me
are twenty-five
thousand days
of Possibilities.

ß07 First Born

He sits in the garden,

back against a tree,

his bottom eclipsed

by the cool grass.

He watches a small thing

run across his foot.

Between his toes

the red clay is still wet.

He rubs some of it

between his fingers

and smells the Spring Earth

with its hint of mint and suckle.

He is alone in the garden
except for the animals
and the butterfly
now resting on his thigh.
He marvels at the wings
in rhythm to his own breathing.

He watches a second creature
watching him watching him.
His mind is clear and fresh;
memories only as old as the day,
a day spent in the cool garden
beneath the baby blue sky.
He had woken beneath a broad tree,
a new man, clean as red cherries.
There are things he wants to say
but he is mute for the moment.
He drinks cold water from the spring
and tastes fresh berries off the bush.
The evening air feels good on his skin.

Later, he reclines in the green grass

and wonders at the night sky in its glory.

He is bewitched by the patterns of stars;

in their distance is a remembrance

that eludes him after only a day.

Around him shade and shadows abound,

and the dark trees are heavy and full.

Round is the fruit yet to be touched

and long the leaves of the unplucked fig.

ß08 Autumn Rise

Between the sun and nightfall comes the glow
of crimson strokes that sweep the daylight by.
The knowing owl appears as bats swoop low;
The moon begins to reign the starling sky.

I rise and leave the sheets, my great escape,
and climb beyond the limbs of tethered tree.
I fly like ghosts who haunt the mortal nape.
The wind she blows; my billowed soul's now free.

I skim the trim of house and chimneyed home,
the smoke like rising prayers that bear no price.
I whisk and whisper round the forest dome
where animals nuzzle the autumn ice.

Below me lies a herd of quiet deer
who watch this vaunted flight of man in fear.

ß09 *Above the Yellowstone*

At two in the morning,

while I am sound asleep,

my brain bursts with color.

The spirit inside me

finds wings in a corner,

straps them on and lifts me.

I see what used to be:

great herds of buffalo

against the rolling Plain

running wild at full speed

while the full rivers pour

over rock not yet smooth.

The forests too are full

and green with virgin life.

The Native Americans

are free to roam the trails.

They are second shadows

to the bear and the deer.

They watch the animals
and breathe in the same air.
There is a mystery
that moves both fish and flesh,
a spark that gives them life.
It intrigues the Native.
The creatures seem to know
their purpose for living;
they embellish the Earth
and walk in God's pleasure.
All around, the sharply
carved mountains speak His will.
Divine power that pushed
and lifted the Rockies,
moved the glaciers northward,
and drew the rivers' course

through vertical canyons
in a rapid motion.
I see the Yellowstone;
its geysers are haunting.
They remind me that Earth
has its own mystery
set in place by the One
who watches over us.
I wake up and wonder
if God is pleased with us.
It is a trembling thought,
and I yearn to return
to mid-millenium,
before my ancestors
had left the English shore
and fired a single shot.

ß10 Boy Natural

My son the natural
calls every little critter
his very best friend,
though the oval roly-polies
are clearly his favorite.
'Buddies,' he calls them.
He finds them everywhere,
all sizes and shades of grey
—even the rarity in blue—
and rescues them from
the fate of a buggy world.
He talks to them, holds them,
lets them crawl among
his fingers and along
his hand. He tires them out.
By morning they are plum
tuckered out from a boy's play.
They are curled up fast asleep,
their short life overnight.

ß11 Aquaternity

I have been drawn inside a whale
and lived there a day or two,
until blown free into the clear
North Pacific brisk morning air.
And I have lived inside of men,
both the good and the evil, though
I am always glad to leave them,
and return to the burgeon-clouds.
To travel on the high currents
and fall as rain, or hail, or snow.
I never know where I will land—
on tree or roof or rustled stream.
I became virgin snow in the Sierras
and lived inside a great Sequoia.
I rose in years three hundred feet;
it was a most breath-taking view.

I touched the ships of Columbus
before he ever reached the New World,
when he was desperate with doubt
that the Earth was round, not flat.
I was part of the ice in the Delaware
when Washington forged across.
I watched the crippled Titanic
slip into the frigid dark-ink
before I rushed into the open lungs
of a scared, abandoned young soul.
Such a far cry from the Ice Age,
with its millennial years of rest
and wait for the liberating sun.
Wild, heady times for the waters,
we formed new and rapid rivers
and carved our name in the rock.

ß12 Soul of a Bug

Twixt sticks and stones
    and the old dog's bones,
Tween twigs and twattle
    and the dung of cattle
slide the snails and slugs
    and all the ordinary bugs.
The common roly-polies,
    those tanks of the forest;
centipedes and millipedes,
    bullet trains of the bush;
horrific crooked spiders
    hanging over crooked paths.

Houseflies and butterflies
> *bumblebees and ladybugs*
glow-worms and slow worms
June bugs and beetle bugs
> *and the cold light fireflies—*
> *greenish dots that never join.*
Then the quicksilver arrives—
> *the double-winged dragons*
> *who dart and dive*
> *twixt twig and hive*
while the white-flannel moths
> *rush to dance the jitter-bug*
> *with drops of the moon*
> *as an orchestra of crickets*
> *plays a spirited tune.*

ß13 Bottled Light

In the shadows
of a dark house
a young boy rests
on his elbows
staring into
a warm glass jar.
In a twilight
he has mirrored
Edison's work—
he's bottled light,
though not as bright
or candent
as the clever
old Inventor.

He's mesmerized
beneath the stars
as he watches
the flickery lights
inside.

They fly and flash
within the jar;
they know they are
trapped;
their wings rise
beneath the lid
but the boy hears

nothing beyond
the cicadas
and the wood frogs
and a hundred
musically-
inclined crickets.

He is oblivious
to anything
that's beyond his
own bottled light.

Not even the
wet grass can move
him from this spot.

He taps the glass
with the pad
of his finger
and the captive
creatures
watch the
mouth move.
It is their first
time
they see a
boy up close.

He is a mild
curiosity
to all of them;
mildly yes, but
they want to go—

back to their fields
and the dark space
that hangs between
the bush and tree.
They want to fly
home and hover
near the crickets
and the clover
and the fragrant
hedge of old rose.

They crawl along
the smooth clear glass,
sending signals
to those still free.
For the boy amused,
it is suspended time,

a night he will
remember long
after the frost
has come and gone
and come again.
Long after he
has found his love
and married
and made little ones
of his very own.

Without asking,
his left hand twists
and frees the lid.
Then all at once,
without a prompt,
the captive lights
rise and spread like
bubble wishes
off a child's wand.

In the cool lift
of the night air
they separate
like the distant
stars above them.

The boy watches
them disappear
into a field
of a thousand
green and amber
lights, and he smiles.
In some small way
they are all now
bound together
in memory
for all time's sake.

ß14 Animate Confetti

I watch as the yellow crepe lands
on my windshield like a speck
that has fallen off of the aging sun.
The paper slowly unfolds itself
like a Chinese fortune after dinner
and reveals a line of jet black life,
its six small prints lightly pressing
into the dusty dirt that marks my view.
The light does indeed turn green again
and with the slowest of starts, I let
the animate confetti rise above me.

ß15 Run of the Mill

Steeple chase
Manhattan
chowder
powder keg
of beer

garden gnome
Alaska
salmon
run of the
mill stone

mountain top
of his game
set, match
book maker
of love.

ß16 *Truth be Known*

Truth is rather

like smoke

in a beehive.

It clouds the air,

stupefies the bees,

obfuscates reality

and alters

the otherwise

healthy dynamics

of a complex society.

We are a nation

of busy bees

content to believe

that all that

needs to be

known is known

and the rest

is like dust

best left alone.

ß17 The Understudy

Oliver, the bachelor,
sits up tight in his box
staring into the limelight.
He lives through the theatre
arriving on time every night
to watch life in three acts.
His heart quickens hearing
the three chimes; he blushes
as the curtain begins to rise.
He enjoys the change of scenery
with its adrenaline rushes
before the lights re-open his eyes.
He relishes the twisted plots
and the ways the characters
move to their marks on cue.
Puppets without any thoughts,
they deliver their lines when due,
with all the dramatic gestures.

They utter lines from memory
while the bachelor in the hall
listens for the odd ad lib or gaffe.
He could be an understudy
were it not for the fourth wall
that separates art from life.
He is comfortable in the dark;
there is no risk in the gallery.
No worries or fear of falling flat.
He is content to hear Juliet hark
from his own distant balcony.
There is no rejection in that.
Let others wait bravely in the wings
and prove how much they want this.
The stars line up for the curtain call.
As they bow and enjoy the fame it brings
(under the diaphanous gaze of Thespis),
Oliver exits House left to nightfall.

ß18 In a Blink

Life happens in a blink,
pivots of a living being
lasting not even a second.
Quiet, visible heartbeats—
more than four hundred
and thirty-five million
between suckle and ashes.
Yet we blink in fear
that life will pass us by.
So we live like grasshoppers
consuming the summer green.
Yes, a few play like crickets,
but they hide in the shadows—
heard but never quite seen.
Even the beauty of the butterfly
fades in the afternoon sun,
as its paper wings fan slowly
until its short month is done.
Then, in a blink it is gone.

ß19 Fortitude of the Morning Frost

It is having

the fortitude

of morning frost,

the conviction

of a wind-caught

parachute seed,

and the long-term

memory of water

that has brought

us to this point.

ƒ20 A Resting Shadow

He is a strange boy
who lives in a broad tree
strung with Japanese lanterns—
green and the primary colors.
Secure in a forked branch,
he reads Shakespeare aloud
as squirrels watch over head.
Romeo, he is not; but he
dreams in the mid-summer
and fancies himself Horatio,
Hamlet's good and loyal friend.
'Ghost' and 'mousetrap,' he mutters
but the tragic play has been rendered.
Pounds of flesh are worth little
when fed by a heart that flutters.
But soon he will wake in early joy,
his soul secured in the argent sky.

.

ß21 Roundabout

sticks in the mud
bath towels—
his and hers that match—

box car
stereo
Jack
And Jill
Ted at the altar
Call

back
Stab in the dark
Circles
Under the eyes
entropic state
of civil discourse
from angry lip

ß22 *A Bubble Off Plumb*

We are a drop
of daylight
in a sea of night.
A ball of wax
in the Milky Way.
softened
by the millennial sun.
A child's marble
spinning
in midair
without help
of kite string
or sleight of hand.
A lightning rod
of thunderstone.

A circus
beneath the cirrus.

Beneath
this cloudy veil
oceans turn
while rivers flow;
mountains age
as grasses grow.
Mammals flee
where fishes go;
mothers grieve
while fathers leave.
Devils brew
as traders sail.
A small ship hugs
the African coast.
All the world s
seeks its name.
Cargo of children,
slaves to men.

ß23 Polka Dot Girl

She twirls around
on the sidewalk
watching herself
in the window.
A cutie-pie
in a polka dot dress—
with the clipped tag
still dangling
from the notched sleeve.
Her wide eyes rest
on her glass face
and cradle smile.
She giggles while
her body wiggles.

She tilts her head
and her eyes swivel
to the grey ground.
She twirls and swirls
on her little-girl heels
while the colored
dots she most adores
rise from the print
and plate-glass front
and leave her past
like bright balloons
that join the sky
all too soon

ß24 *Popinjay*

"All

the world's

a stage"—

our own

soapbox

we carry

around

with us

from place

to place

and all

the points

that lay

between.

There is

a bit

of vanity

in each

of us,

a lingering

by the mirror

to adjust

the hair,

or check

the teeth

for currant

or errant

poppyseed

before we

turn around

and begin

to babble on

about this

or that

with little

thought for

him or her,

it or them

ß25 Box of Snakes!

"Box of Snakes!"
she says
so as not to swear.
She is mindful of her
P's and Q's,
though I wonder
what she would say
if she knew it stood
for pints and quarts.

She is a woman
of gentle means.
She prays
for butterflies on
cold nights,
and washes her

hydrangeas after
the Santa Anas leave.
She dresses ten
years beyond her age
in conservative
prints and flowers.
She has a good soul,
speaking as she does
well inside her
box of snakes.

ß26 *Grumblebutt*

In my house

we have a name

for those

who rise

up on the wrong

side of the bed:

Grumblebutt.

Three syllables

of grumpy hell.

No sense hiding

the annoyance

of a funky mood.

Just blow through

the house

like a Kansas

twister.

Let the others
know you're there
and couldn't care
less
whether you're down
or sunny side up.
Just trudge on through
with your monkeys blue,
and don't let
the door
leave your Grumbles
behind.

ß27 Hai-Jacked

Romney Obama
catering to rich favors
political pie

Green paper ticket
the sale of the century
Lincoln's own bedroom

Open ballot box
Secrets of the smoke-filled room
Nothing is for free

High cost of living
Discordant civil discourse
Shrinking middle class

ß28 *Star Struck*

We wonder about Pluto
and what lies
beyond the Milky Way.
We lose sleep
counting a b'zillion stars
with names like AC43.
We wander blindly about
tripping over the fallen trees
that were Yesterday's success.
We find nothing there
in the open space.
Lots of light but little shape.

ß29 Frog Skins

Librae-Solidi-denarii. Pounds-Shillings-Pence.
Eight farthings to a tuppence.
Three tuppence to a tanner.
Two tanners to a shilling—a bob.
Five shilling to a crown—twenty to a pound.
A Sovereign of gold; a quid in paper.
A million pounds, pure Marigold; quid pro quo.
Thick brass Maggies in modern coin.
British dosh and lolly to mind your p's and q's.
Across the pond we live on frog skins.
Greenbacks, bread and cabbage, dead presidents.
Bucks and sawbucks. Nickels, dimes & the red cent.
C-Notes and smackers. Bones and two-bits,
and the odd Loony that finds its way South
under the mattress and into the cookie jar.
Remember Hamilton, Bob's your uncle.

£8/15s/12d

ß30 *Sweet Pea*

tulips rose, redbuds bloom;
sweet william's morning glory.
Jasmine leaves her sweet perfume
on the limbs of every pear.
Bradford pines for Cythia
where foxtails line the fence.
Before the pig squeaks
and the dogwood bark
the catnips and dragon snaps grow.
Holly envies Lily, thin as a twig,
with her bright, mum friends so big.
Poor black-eyed Susan still struggles
to beguile the social butterflies
while the more impatient Ivy
climbs the rung of Jacob's ladder.
Near the patch of pussy willows,
strong Johnny jumps up and gives
his ox-eyed Daisy her hearts ease
before pulling the black nightshade.

ß31 unsettled

When I was a kid in the Sixties,

we saw the country in black and white.

There was little grey.

Color television was still a thing of wonder.

The mainstream had one voice,

a general view of right and wrong.

Today, my country 'tis of thee

is no longer a civil union

of red, white, and blue.

We are red or blue or purple,

but mostly red and blue.

Our collective, national character—

Lincoln's 'mystic chords' that bind us—

has been frayed by years of neglect.

So, now, we live on the slippery slopes

of Itsallaboutme & Imgonnadowhatiwannado.

Land of the Greed and the Home of the Rogue.

52

ß32 Elementary

I drew life out of the box,
colored folk and Crayola white—
pigments of an imagination
that I carried to paper.
They echoed the voice I gave them,
sixty-four shades of diverse beauty,
newness, struggle, and weakness.
Rapt figures that didn't talk back
but were drawn to their animation.

ß33 *C-G-A-T Spells* Man

It is strange,

is it not,

that the number

and placement

of four letters—

A, T, C, and G

on twisted nano-

ladders of DNA—

determine

the look and feel,

complexion

and complexity

of us all?

The granularity

of green in our eyes;

the red and blue

in the hue of our blood;
the black and yellow
in our hair;
the snow or
the glow on our head;
the flavor and freckles
of our skin.
Five feet or six feet
on top of the two;
elephant ears
or cowlicked hair;
rosy cheeks—
both top and bottom!
sharp mind or flat feet;
cold feet or hot head.
Blue spirits or yellow spine;
Generous or not so kind.

Barrel chest or Roman nose;
virile strength or cloven-toes.
Smooth skin or beastly back.
Strong or prone
to heart attack.
MS or ALS;
high IQ or déjá vu.

Grey matter
and white matter
Does all the other
really matter?

ß34 Red Light. Green Light.

It was a popular
game to play
in my day:
Run forward
without
getting caught.
Now I believe
we live
as we are taught.
Red light. Green light.
Spend now,
pinch later.
I read once
it takes an ounce
of ink,
green and black,
to print a single
buck.

Penny wise
and pound foolish,
we spend a dollar
seventy-one
for every dollar
carried in.
Two point five
million dollars
of red ink
every minute—
an unsustainable pace
by all accounts.
We ignore the obvious
and assume we are
much too big to fail.
But one day,
if we don't change,
we might find
ourselves
bank-possessed and

Up for Sale.

Red light.

ß35 *The Goggle Box*

Along the length of the street
I can see the blue glow
in every window
as house after house
has turned off the porch light
and darkened the Welcome mat,
leaving the poor moths
to fend for themselves.

I pass the first house.
The yellow Cottage is glued
to ESPN and soccer:
Mexico 3, Argentina 2.
The Colonials are absorbed
in The History Channel.
Their youngest died in a war.
The Cape Cods Want
to be a Millionaire

while two doors down the Tudors
are in the middle of a Family Feud.
The white Pickets are studying
This Old House.
Blueprints line their floor.

The Wraparounds have found
My Favorite Martian beside Mr. Ed.
At the corner of Friends, Everybody
loves Raymond and the Naked Chef.
As the Clapboards Diagnose Murder,
the A-frame is hooked on the A-Team.
The Gables are in Seventh Heaven;
The Brick & Mortars are set for Survivor.
Next door the pink Victorian
is living in the middle of Mayberry,
and the Stuccos are in Stuckeyville.

The widowed Bungalow

can't decide between CNN and Discovery.

The Stones are in Providence again.

Duplex Left is being Touched by an Angel

while the Right is in the Twilight Zone.

Spanish style is out, while the Verandas

soak up the intrigue of the West Wing.

It's a Bonanza on Broadway.

By the time I reach the bottom of the hill,

I Get Smart, grab a Taxi, and head to Cheers.

ẞ36 *A Colorful Life*

Albugineous. Columbine. Niveous.

Blessed be the rows of Arlington stone.

Coccineous. Incarnadine. Sanguineous.

Blessed be the heroes who stand alone.

Luteous. Jacinthe. Melichrous.

Blessed be our days of flesh and bone.

Citreous. Meline. Flammeous.

Blessed be the mentors who raise the child.

Vitreous. Smaragdine. Chlorochrous.

Blessed be the defenders of the wild.

Cyaneous. Mazarine. Porphyrous.

Blessed be the meek and the mild.

Puniceous. Amaranthine. Violaceous.

Blessed be those with eternal goals.

Brunneous. Sarcoline. Aeneous.

Blessed be the dust beneath their soles.

Piceous. Nigrine. Atrous.

Blessed be the spirits of the departed souls.

ß37 Hai-Finance

Dollars on credit
Bubbles into deficits—
The Great Recession

George W. Bush
On the brink of disaster
Two thousand and eight.

Dollar pounds euro.
Gold in ground; paper abounds.
Money moves the world.

ß38 *Fireflies*

Summer spots of green
Here tonight, gone tomorrow
Cold sparks of fire

ß39 Broken Spellbound

Precocious Perspicuity.

A rush to judgment.

Perspicuity Obscurity.

It's as clear as mud.

Loquacious Elocution.

William Jefferson Clinton.

Truculent Succulent.

Prickly cactus.

Pabulum Incunabulum.

Mother's milk.

Vitreous Albugineous.

Egg white.

Maximus Mumpsimus.

Rush Limbaugh.

Dendrophileous Chlorochorus.

Tree hugger.

Farrago Imbroglio.

FUBAR.

Logorrhea Diarrhea.

Loose lips.

Mazarine. Mezzanine.

The royal box at Albert Hall.

Cyaneous Sanguineous.

Blue blood.

Pushkin's Withershins.

Counter-revolutionary.

ß40 A Block of Ice

On the back porch
the man lay the ice down.
A single block of ice
sweating as much
as the man
who labored the hill.
Drips in tandem race
down the slippery face

As a boy
he worked in the ice house
along with his father
and four brothers.
All are gone
and only the pit
of the house remains.

He sits on a crate
and rests,
watching the ice melt,
its puddle edging
toward his feet.
Soon the cool water
will wash his soles.

He seems mesmerized
by the little block of glacier.
He knows they come out
of a machine on the corner now.
The days of the sunken house
and the straw floors are gone.

By the time he leaves,
the ice is half-gone.

There is a deep bow
in the top
where a man could sit
and cool his heels.
But he is ready to go.

The time has gone fast.
The puddle is now a shallow
lake that covers the dried punch.
The ice has curves now;
it is in the prime of its life.

But he knows it's time to go.
For a final time he sweeps
his hand along the smooth glass.
He drinks the little water
that comes in his hand
and leaves the rest to gather
around the matron's steps.

ß41 Lady of Marlborough

She models in the nude,
fixated on a point
to make it be nothing.
She is aware, but not,
that those in clothes must stare
at her every choice curve,
her oval shapes and mound.
It is the face they tend
to leave some other time,
a conscious nervousness
that it might be for art—
for all the right reasons—
but that very deep down
they remain the voyeur
of their adolescence,
their manly pens leaking
wet for the still marble
girl on the pedestal.

ß42 Dead Cat Sleeping

On High Street
between the broken white
line there lay a cat.
A tabby cat.
Motionless. Frozen
from the night air.
His tail rising
with each passing car.

Only a cat
could be so divorced
from the world
to nap in the middle
of a pockmarked road.
So confident
to recover from a hard
night by resting
on a hard road.

He slumbers

as the rest of us lumber.

By morning he will be gone.

And all of us will

be left to wonder:

Was he pressed into service

by a hard-nosed truck?

Devoured by the dogs?

Carried away by Sanitation?

Buried by the homeless?

Did the Gremlins rush

him off to Hell?

Or did he simply rise

from the asphalt

in the dead of night

and assume his penultimate

Life.

Where do the dead cats go?

ß43 Slippers

She slipped quietly away this night,
her soul walking on the rafters.
In the room she left behind
a body she had worn so well.
First as a baby at her mother's breast;
then as a little girl in a pretty pink dress.
A cherub plucked from the sky,
she toddled with her doll in hand.

Every old woman was once a skipping girl.
Skin, smooth and clear, auburn hair.
A mouth of baby teeth and tiny voice.
She held tea parties in the green shade
and nursed the owies of her ragged girl.
She conversed with the inanimate folk
and shared the stories in her Papa's lap.

Every old woman was once a giggling girl.
Eyes peeking behind the smile.
Watching the older boys play ball
or ride their bikes high off the curb.

She held her own in the dating game
and danced often in the open air,
though in the blink of a passing bike
she slipped into womanhood.

The years fly by so fast
 and at last her three gems
have left the shadow of the nest.
She spends the nights
with her husband on the porch
watching shooting stars
and cars drive by.
She is in the twilight,
and the nights are longer.

And colder still the night
her husband slipped away,
as quietly as their first dance
in the park that early May.

She is happy now to go herself
but wonders how it is that life
could run its course so fast;
how eighty years of memories
could all be packed in her mind.
Boxed up tight and yet she moves
from year to year with the grace
of a ballet girl in the green shade.

She spends her final day
among the bushes,
sons and daughters of the first
plantings of an early marriage.
She rests in the swing
and remembers when

her husband painted the house last.
She can almost see the brush strokes.

It is a hot day,
not unlike when she was a little girl.
Strange how this day brings her
back to her youth.
Her mind moves backwards
as the day wears on.
By nightfall she is a young girl
again, sharing a pillow with her doll.

She is ready to skip again,
and anxious to hold her Papa's hand.
She can almost taste the lemonade
her Mother is surely making.
She smiles when she thinks of her man.
Her fingers tingle at the idea of his clasp.
How long she has longed for him.

As the rest of life moves forward a day,

she slips quietly out of the house,

leaving behind slippers of dusty rose.

ß44 Night-Light

The light still shines in the corner of the Ark

as Noah reads a tale to his two little Pigs.

Old Jonah still smells like the belly of the Whale,

who in the deep exhales his wailing songs.

The Lion foxtrots feisty with his tasseled tail,

as the others run loose in the drizzled dark.

While the hunters roam, the rest run home

to the light that shines in the corner of the room.

ß45 Baton Rouge

A glass in a stick
sits level on my desk.
An orange cut of wood
from a place in Omaha.
It has the line markings
of a ruler on its side
counting up to a dozen
from far left to right.
But on top center sits
the bubble in the glass.
Focused center stage.
A slight tilt and it rises
like the breath of a fish.

When my Grampa left
the Earth, it was this
simple block of wood
and water I wanted most.
Elements of a living tree.
It set on a shelf in his shop
beside manly tools, grease
and oil, and pencil stubs
trimmed only by a knife
in the hand of an old farmer.
He was a hard, exact man
who raised both pigs and corn
in the corner of Minnesota.

While others sought more
treasured things from his past,
I seized the level quickly
like it was a baton in the race.
My heart jumped as his stopped.
I looked forward as he stepped
back to watch me carry the flame.
This simple symbol of the torch,
with its ability to measure both
distance and stability.
Balance and progress combined.
For fifty years he kept it near,
first in the barn and then in town.

Now it is in my house at Panadrew.

A good reminder of the measure

of a good and honest man, I am sure.

It is a connection from one man

to another, one generation

to another; from a rural nation

to an urban suburban creation.

This simple piece of wood has value

because it was his, because he held

it in his hand and used it, and looked

through the same glass window

and saw the lively little bubble move

left and right in a world all its own.

ß46 *Still Life*

He grabs a paper for comfort;
he will wear it inside his shirt
to insulate him from the chill
of early Spring's air of new birth.
For him, the days have little worth;
just space before his life stands still.

ƒ47 Debits & Credits

Bigger Government.
The Age of Bureaucracy—
Budget deficits.

Debits and credits.
Language of the accountants.
Void of emotion.

Tax breaks for the rich,
the shaft for the middle class,
pennies for the poor.

Buy now, pay later.
Mortgage our children's future.
Soon we speak Chinese.

ß48 American Dream

Beyond inflation.
An economic time bomb.
College tuition.

The suburban house:
financial freedom behind
the white picket fence.

Direct deposit.
Work house. gas cars. clothes. food stuff:
Paycheck to paycheck.

From cradle to grave
We work, save, spend; build, live, give.
American dream.

ß49 *Passendia*

In the arrival of a new sky,
when Earthly shadows pale to God,
life arrives in many shades
through rush of air and hearty cry.

We grow slowly while days fly fast;
run and play in the light of day.
The Noon hour leaves Morning past;
We're told to put our toys away.

We rush through life's frantic drive
but Twilight's past; the moon is high.
Younger souls will soon arrive
as older whispers must say goodbye.

Embers from the torch still burn;
in memory's way we come again.
Passersby will have their turn
to wander past and wonder when.

ß50 Days of the Departed

Gone are the days
    of open windows and candlesticks;
hissy needles on jet black wax;
    mild manners and the mild retort.
Gone are the clotheslines
    of billowing sheets and flapping socks;
Uncle Wiggily and the little poor fox;
    landlines and post-marked letters;
Sundays closed and beds of feathers;
    the domed cage and the vintage hat box.
Gone are the inkwells,
    the shaved goose quill, and the royal wax seal.
Bye the calm and measured words.
    Thank you. Sir. Ma'am, and Please.
Gone are the men in starched shirts
    and creased dress hats;
paper bags and the paper boys,
    glassblowers and the glass pop bottles,
    and evenings filled with porch-swing chats.

ß51 Mirabel

She washes windows for a living,

spending her day on a wooden ladder

where people walk an arc around her.

She is as transparent as the glass she cleans.

Necessary but unnoticed; she is muted,

though she presses on with her own dream.

She sweeps the squeegee through soapy

water and wipes the pane dry and clear.

She works robotically for those on the ground

but her own piece of mind is already far away

in the apricot orchards of her native Florence.

She smiles as she reaches for the grooved

orange fruit and smells its blushed fragrance.

She wipes the sticky, sweet juice from her chin

and fills her bucket with the golden gems.

In pockets flagged with rags, she slips

a pit or two to plant for better times

when she is again among the seen and heard

and life is more than a mere reflection.

ß52 Eyescape

Night falls.

I rise.

Bats break

wind in

jagged

hurried

food flights

as geese

cross the

sky in

leisure.

The grey

squirrels

rush to

gather

Summer

before

it leaves.

I sip

merlot

and watch

a deer

watch me.

This lawn

is home.

Rabbits

robins,

pin oak,

dogwood,

cedar.

The deer

and skunk

alike.

My swing,

my Self.

Content,

tonight

I will

dream with

both eyes

open.

ß53 The Birds and the Bees

If not for the bees, there would be no fruit
for the birds to eat and carry the seed.
If not for the seeds, there would be no root
or rising shoot for the flowers that feed.
Rejoice in the birds and the busy bees
who live together in the nestled trees.
If we buy the birds and bury the bees,
who makes the music in the evening breeze?
Who spreads the color on the gentle green?
Who grows the refuge for the rook and queen?
Rejoice in the birds and the busy bees
who live together in the nestled trees.

ß54 Iced Coffee and Haute Coiffure

We live in the days of later,

beyond the haven of the garden

with its long, cool shadows

and cold, cherished fruit.

We toil in the modern ways—

über-impersonal, practical,

secular, and metrosexual.

We spend our extended lives

in the long lines of service needs:

Coffee iced and nice coiffure;

Flavored and sculptured looks;

Pluck and tuck to roll back time.

We seek first the fleshed pleasures

that remind us we are most alive,

until we become utterly lost

in the temporal realm of all-about-me.

Hey, can I super-size that for you?

ß55 A Parliament of Owls

I was born on October 20, 1959
and on that warm Autumn day
the Earth was teeming with animals:
beds of clams and towers of giraffes;
prides of lions and prickles of porcupines;
pods of whales and streaks of tigers;
a knot of toads and a parliament of owls;
shivers of sharks and nests of snakes;
braces of ducks and murders of crows;
colonies of bats and covies of quail;
a romp of otters and warrens of rabbits.
It was a diverse troop of engaging life:
musters and murmurations; cackles
and smacks; and grand convocations
near the lilting exaltations of the larks.

By New Year's Day, 1960
every fly alive that October day
had already returned to microdust
in the brown grass of Winter.
They have replenished themselves,
along with the birds and the bees,
many times over, but those who
fluttered and flew on my first day
are long gone in the natural course.
So is every dog and cat and mouse.
The lobsters and the golden lions
followed suit the day I drove a car.
The last of the 1959 black bear
left this Earth in my freshman year
of college in the Blue Ridge of Virginia.
By graduation, the polar bears were
gone too, along with the gorillas
and the horses, both tame and wild.

The grizzlies lasted to my mid-twenties;
the bald eagle and the hippos made
it to the day I stepped into my thirties.

I was forty when the last Asian elephant
followed his mother's distant tracks.
Now there are just a few who were alive
before I took my first breath and cried.
The Elatus parrot and the Andean condor
and both the blue and the killer whale,
and the oldest of all, the patient turtle
who long ago outlived the frisky hare.
How sad it is to know that most every
living creature from my first day of life
is now gone in the natural course of things
before I had a chance to really say good-bye.

ß56 *Everyone Sleeps*

The stars shine

whether we see them or not,

whether we are in the mood or not.

The world goes on,

even when we want it to stop

so we can catch our breath.

The Earth is an impossible engine;

it stops for no one and no thing.

Even the famous must close

their eyes and sleep for a little while

while the world moves on.

No one can stay awake forever,

and we all have one thing in common:

Every day, whether we like it or not,

our unique bodies are all a day older.

We are each closer to the inevitable—

our own specific time when we will

close our eyes for the very last time.

It is the great humanizer and protector.

ß57 Night Watch

In the middle of the ocean
past the parting of the sun
but hours before the stars
will venture from the dark,
the Host of all peers down from Heaven.
He leans toward the blue wilderness
until He is just a whisker's width
from water that rocked the ancient ark.
His divine breathe hangs as steam
above the husky dusky matter
as He looks far down the ocean floor.
Making the water into His image,
He presses His face down into it.
Brightest eyes light
up the darkest depth.
Beacons beckon the living
to the top at the water's edge.

He hears the whales

through miles of liquid life.

Dolphins race toward His face;

turtles and rays, and fish of prey;

squid and eel, sword and seal.

sea lion and horse and every otter soul.

Decapods and octopods.

Shrimp and prawn and octopi.

flying fish and jellyfish;

sturgeon, bass, and sole,

Masses now teeming rising to the top

to hear the eminent Fisher's call.

He lifts His head from the salty sea;

brow and chin above the spray.

As water falls from His majestic face,

a billion eyes spot His grace.

Cheek and chin now a fathom high,

He raises His head toward a speckled sky.

ß58 Amen

You drew me
from the deep,
from the dark deep
of the unborn night.
You raised me
to be upright,
accustomed
to the morning light.
You brace me
against the wind
and the salty waves
of rocky shores.
You hold me
tight as storms arrive
on darkish days
and let me drink
the cup of rain.

You lift me
up in quiet time
and rock me soon
to perfect peace.

About the Poet Lumijnfroost

Timothy Ray Phillips, aka Phineas Lumijnfroost, grew up in the Amish country of Lancaster County, Pennsylvania. Here he found his poetic heart and began writing poetry at the age of thirteen. The small Moravian town of Lititz was a perfect backdrop for Timothy's earliest poems. Much of his work reflects his experience and affinity for small town America.

At seventeen Timothy moved South and began college at Virginia Tech in Blacksburg, Virginia. He graduated cum laude with a Bachelor's degree in Accounting. In addition, he holds a Masters in Business Administration from Azusa Pacific University in California. He is both a Certified Public Accountant (CPA) and a Certified Internal Auditor (CIA). Currently, he is the Controller for a digital ad agency in Blacksburg, Virginia (who says you can't go home?). He jokes that he balances numbers by day and words by night. Peer Lumijnfroost is an admitted night owl and it is in the small hours that his most creative work surfaces.

In addition to writing poetry, Timothy has penned a handful of novels that provide a nice counter-balance to the old television set in the basement. The Ark of Lumijnfroost *is his third book of poetry.*

Timothy, his wife Debbie, and their three teen-aged children live in the beautiful Ellett Valley just east of Blacksburg. Their beached ark includes two lemon-white beagles, two rabbits, two parakeets and, at last count, twenty-three wild deer.

Index

R

S

T

U

W

Timothy Ray Phillips

www.ingramcontent.com/pod-product-compliance
Lightning Source LLC
Chambersburg PA
CBHW051812040426
42446CB00007B/629